EASY PIANO

HOW WE DO )

...PLUS 11 MORE TOP HITS

Published by
Wise Publications
14-15 Berners Street, London W1T 3LJ, UK.

Exclusive Distributors:

Music Sales Limited
Distribution Centre, Newmarket Road,
Bury St Edmunds, Suffolk IP33 3YB, UK.

Music Sales Pty Limited
Units 3-4, 17 Willfox Street, Condell Park
NSW 2200, Australia.

Order No. AM1006027
ISBN: 978-1-78038-874-8
This book © Copyright 2012 Wise Publications,
a division of Music Sales Limited.

Edited by Jenni Norey.

Printed in the EU.

Your Guarantee of Quality:
As publishers, we strive to produce every book
to the highest commercial standards.
This book has been carefully designed to minimise awkward page turns
and to make playing from it a real pleasure.
Particular care has been given to specifying acid-free, neutral-sized paper
made from pulps which have not been elemental chlorine bleached.
This pulp is from farmed sustainable forests and was produced
with special regard for the environment.
Throughout, the printing and binding have been planned to ensure a sturdy,
attractive publication which should give years of enjoyment.
If your copy fails to meet our high standards, please inform us
and we will gladly replace it.

www.musicsales.com

WISE PUBLICATIONS
part of The Music Sales Group
London / New York / Paris / Sydney / Copenhagen / Berlin / Madrid / Hong Kong / Tokyo

BLACK HEART • STOOSHE • 3

GOOD TIME • OWL CITY FEAT. CARLY RAE JEPSEN • 6

HALL OF FAME • THE SCRIPT • 10

HOW WE DO (PARTY) • RITA ORA • 22

LITTLE TALKS • OF MONSTERS AND MEN • 26

PRINCESS OF CHINA • COLDPLAY FEAT. RIHANNA • 15

READ ALL ABOUT IT, PART III • EMELI SANDÉ • 30

SKINNY LOVE • BIRDY • 34

SPECTRUM • FLORENCE + THE MACHINE • 38

SUMMERTIME IN THE CITY • SCOUTING FOR GIRLS • 43

THIS IS LOVE • WILL.I.AM FEAT. EVA SIMONS • 52

WE ARE NEVER EVER GETTING BACK TOGETHER • TAYLOR SWIFT • 48

Black Heart

Words & Music by Shaznay Lewis, Iyiola Babalola,
Darren Lewis & Jo Perry

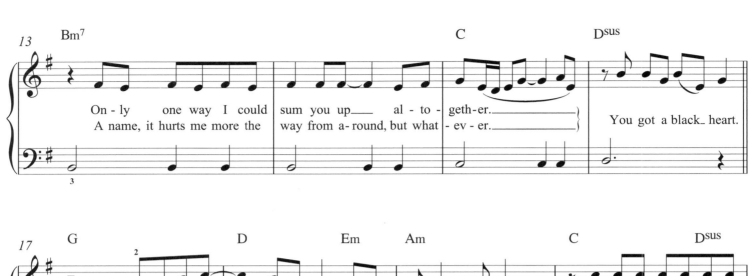

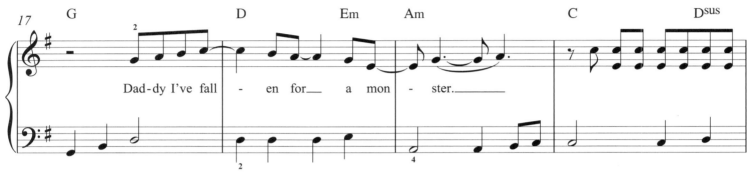

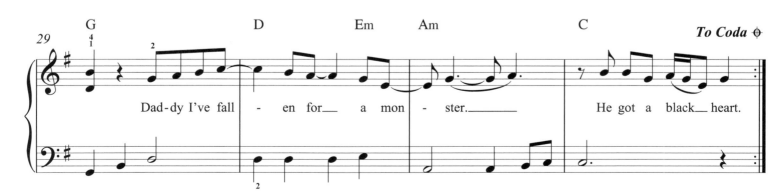

4

Good Time

Words & Music by Adam Young, Brian Dong Ho Lee
& Matthew Thiessen

Hall Of Fame

Words & Music by Mark Sheehan, Daniel O'Donoghue,
will.i.am & James Barry

hands up. You can beat the clock. You can move a moun-tain. You can break rocks. You could be a
peo - ple. Do it for your pride. Nev - er gon-na know if you nev-er e-ven try. Do it for your

mas - ter, don't wait for luck. De - di - cate your -self and you could find your-self.
count-ry. Do it for your name. 'Cause there gon - na be a day when you're..... Stand-ing in the hall of fame.

And the world's__ gon-na know your name.__

'Cause you burn__ with the bright - est flame.__

11

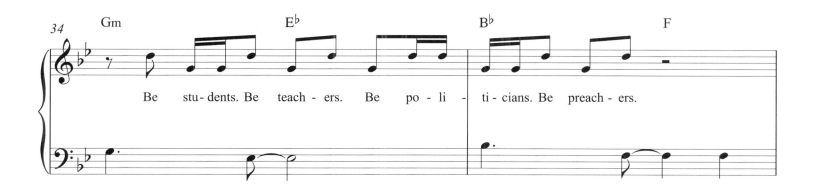

Be stu- dents. Be teach- ers. Be po- li - ti - cians. Be preach- ers.

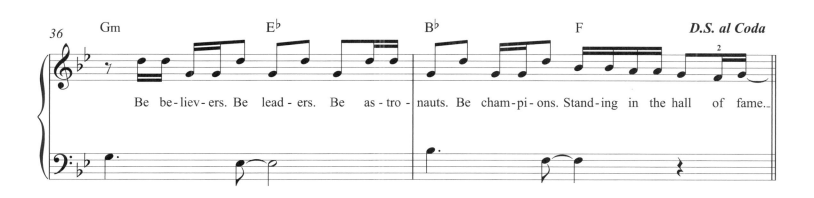

D.S. al Coda

Be be- liev- ers. Be lead- ers. Be as- tro- nauts. Be cham- pi- ons. Stand- ing in the hall of fame..

Coda

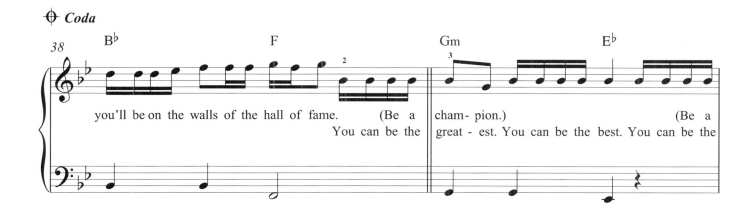

you'll be on the walls of the hall of fame. (Be a cham- pion.) (Be a
You can be the great- est. You can be the best. You can be the

cham- pion.) (Be a cham- pion.) (Be a
King Kong bang- ing on your chest. You could beat the world. You could beat the war. You could talk to

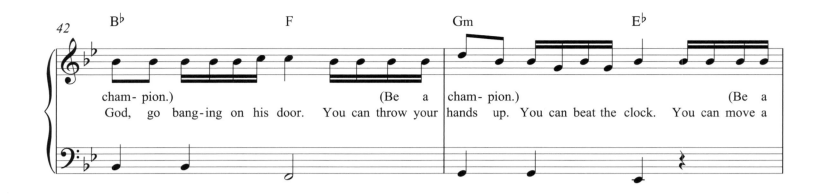

cham- pion.)   (Be   a   cham- pion.)   (Be   a

God,   go   bang-ing on his door.   You can throw your   hands   up. You can beat the clock.   You can move a

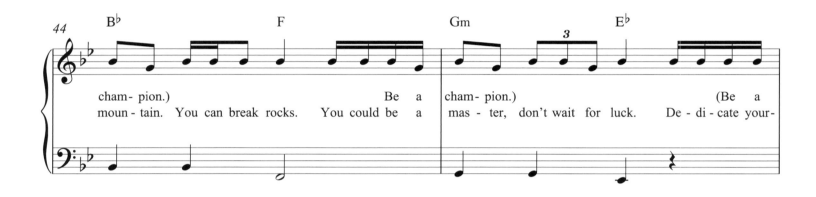

cham- pion.)   Be   a   cham- pion.)   (Be   a

moun- tain. You can break rocks.   You could be   a   mas - ter, don't wait for luck.   De - di - cate your-

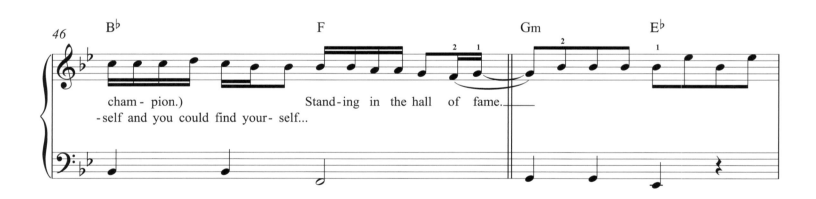

cham - pion.)   Stand-ing   in   the   hall   of   fame.

-self and you could find your- self...

Princess Of China

Words & Music by Chris Martin, Guy Berryman,
Jon Buckland, Will Champion & Brian Eno

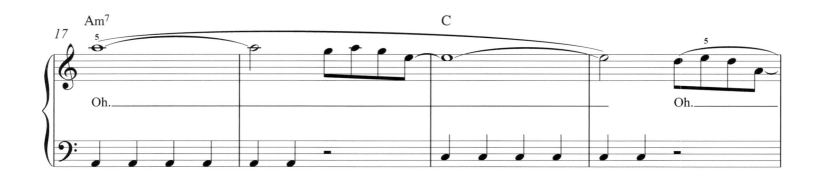

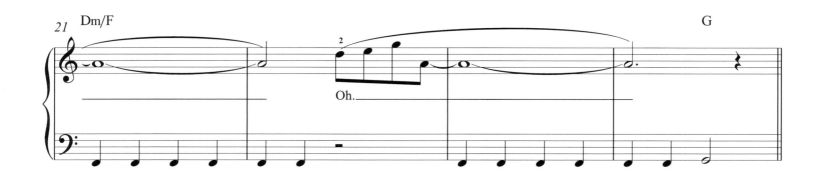

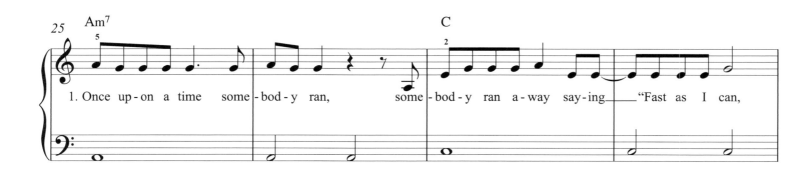

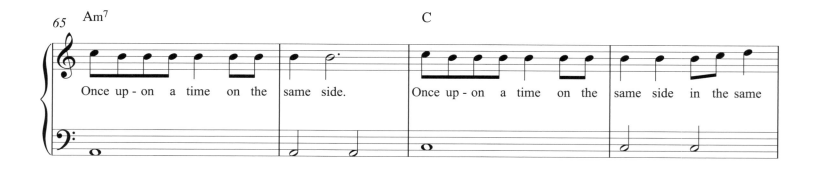

you let me go. I

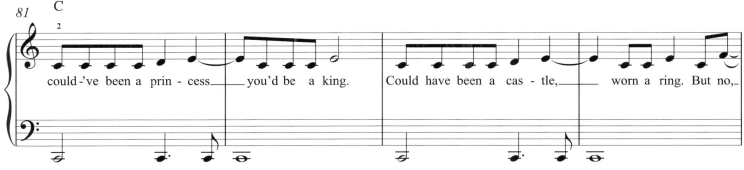

could-'ve been a prin - cess you'd be a king. Could have been a cas - tle, worn a ring. But no,_

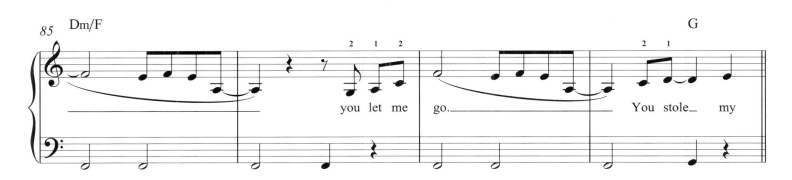

you let me go. You stole_ my

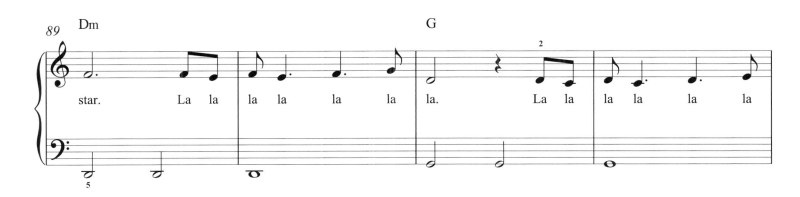

star. La la la la la la la. La la la la la la

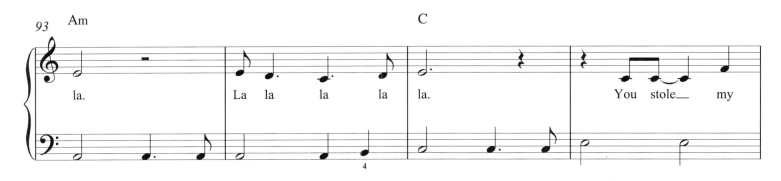

la. La la la la la. You stole_ my

How We Do (Party)

Words & Music by Hal David, Willie Hutch, Bob West, Jermaine Jackson, Bonnie McKee, Christopher Wallace, Andrew Harr, Alexander Delicata, Berry Gordy Jr., Osten Harvey, Kelly Sheehan, Andre Davidson & Sean Davidson

23

Little Talks

Words & Music by Ragnar Thorhallsson & Nanna Bryndis Hilmarsdottir

Read All About It, Part III

Words & Music by Shahid Khan & Emeli Sandé

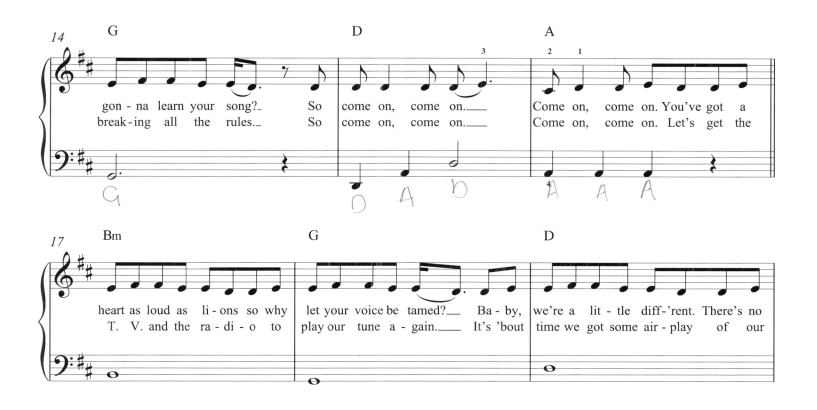

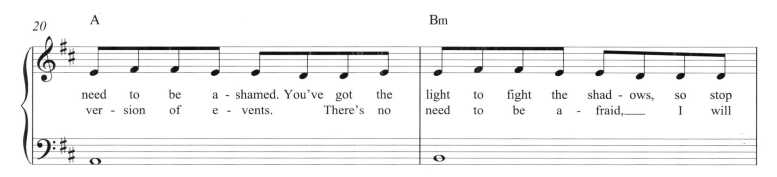

33

Skinny Love

Words & Music by Justin Vernon

hold-ing all___ the tick-ets   and you'll be own-ing all___ the fines.___
break-ing at___ the brit-ches   and at the ends of all___ your lines.___

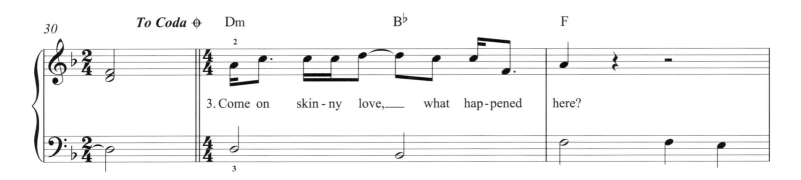

3. Come on   skin-ny love,___   what hap-pened   here?

Suck-le   on the hope in   lite bras - siere.___   My my   my,   my my   my, my my my___ my my.

___   Sul-len   load is   full,___   so slow   on___ the spit.___   And I

♦ Coda

Who will love you?   Who will fight?   And who will   fall_____

Spectrum

Words & Music by Paul Epworth & Florence Welch

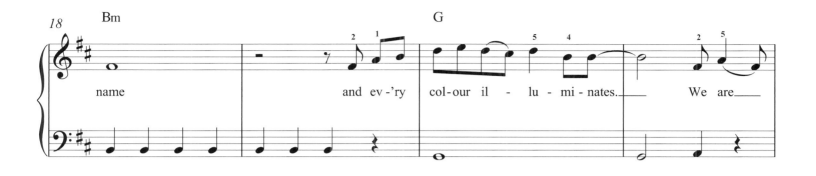

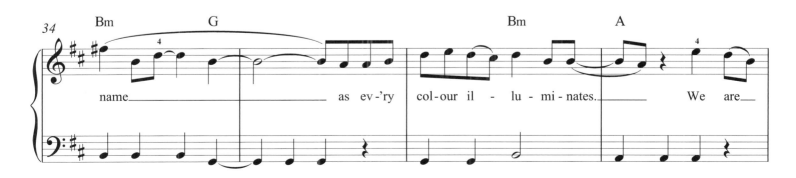

39

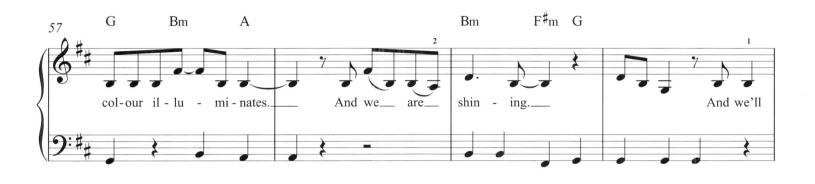

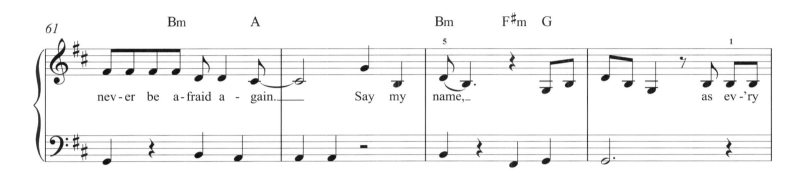

D.S. al Coda

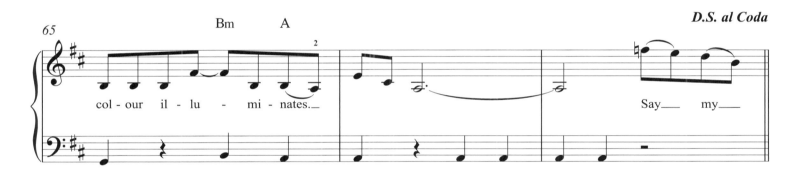

Coda

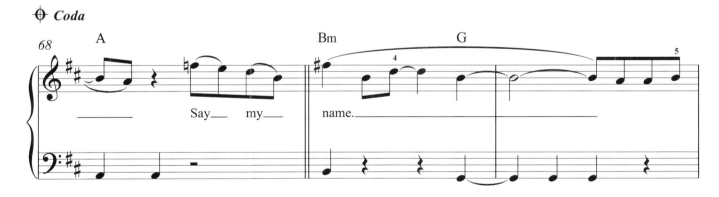

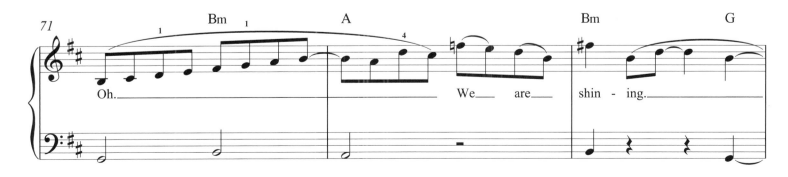

41

Oh. Say my

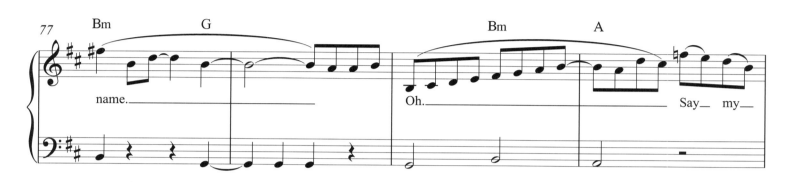

name. Oh. Say my

name. And we'll nev-er be a-fraid a-gain.

Summertime In The City

Words & Music by Roy Stride

We Are Never Ever Getting Back Together

Words & Music by Max Martin, Taylor Swift & Shellback

This Is Love

Words & Music by William Adams, Martin Max, Sebastian Ingrosso,
Eva Simons, Mike Hamilton & Steve Angello

hell,   yeah.   (Hell,   yeah.) Say   hell,   yeah.   (Hell,   yeah.) And say

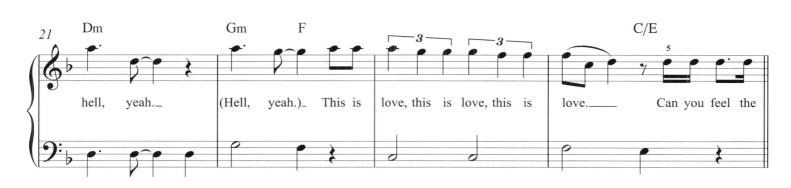

hell,   yeah.   (Hell,   yeah.) This is   love, this is love, this is   love.   Can you feel the

love?   Can you feel the love?   Can you feel the

To Coda

love?   This is   love, this is love, this is   love.

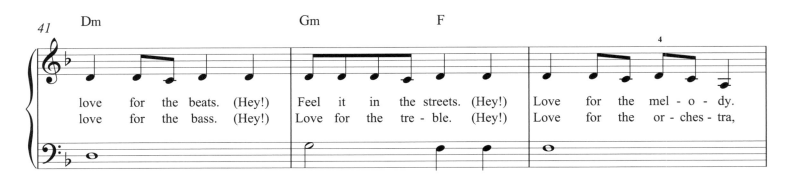

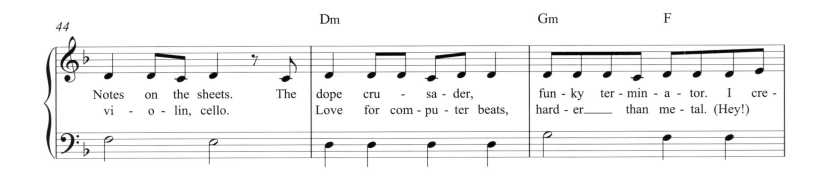

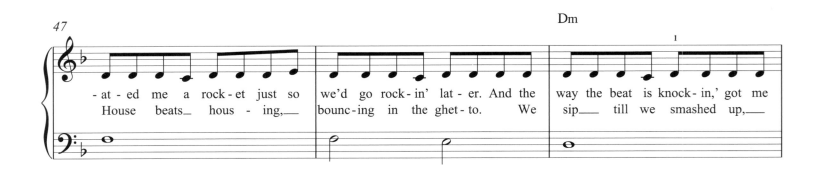

123456789